Why do we sell low and buy high?

The guide you must read BEFORE you invest

Amir Avitzur

ISBN: 0-6155-9107-8
ISBN-13: 9780615591070

Dedication

This book is dedicated to Sharon, Tom, and Royee, my three pillars.

Contents

Introduction—Let the journey begin

We all know that in order to be a successful investor, we should buy low and sell high. In other words, we should pay a low price for our investment and sell it for a higher price. So why do many of us do exactly the opposite? Why do we buy high and sell low?

To answer this question, I would like you to join me on a journey. As you read this book, you will realize some of the major mistakes we make as investors. You will discover why being liked does not make you a good investor, why our inability to not act might stop us from achieving the success we want, and why 88 percent of Swedish drivers believe they are safer drivers than most.

After we learn to recognize some of our mistakes as investors, we will go on to learn about the stock market and the psychology of its participants. You'll learn the true value of a company and that a stock is more than a ticker running at the bottom of a TV screen while an assortment of noises tells you what to do next. You may be surprised to learn that there isn't a single company ticker or even an actual company name mentioned in this book. However, many characteristics of good companies are discussed.

I will share with you the potent thoughts of some of the greatest investors of the last hundred years—luminary people such as Benjamin Graham, Warren Buffett, and Charles Munger. You will learn about the three key areas to explore before acquiring shares of any company. You will also learn about an old man sitting under an olive tree with a wise lad, discussing the fundamentals of valuing a company.

I wrote this book because I believe understanding the fundamentals of investing is a crucial first step in making the right investment decisions, which today more than ever is mandatory for any investor who cares about his or her financial future.

I wrote this book also because I have seen too many people jump in to commit their hard-earned money without knowing the basics of investments, making the same mistakes over and over again and ending up with unsatisfactory results and even frustration about investing. I want you to know more.

This will be the first step in a long and enjoyable journey, during which you will learn how to think about yourself as an investor, some of the checklists you'll need to go through when investing, and how to find a suitable investment at the right price.

I hope that by the time you finish this book you will be as enthusiastic as I am about continuing your education and the lifelong journey of being a value investor.

Live long and prosper,
Amir Avitzur

Chapter 1
Why do we sell low and buy high?

We're often told that in order to be a successful investor we need to buy stock at a low price and sell it at a higher price. If we do that multiple times, we are destined to be rich. Why is it then that so many of us do the exact opposite?

My intention in this chapter is to have us open our minds and address some key questions we seldom ask ourselves. Reflect upon your answers and consider what they reveal about you as an investor.

Which of the following sentences applied to you a few minutes or days before you purchased a stock or shares of a mutual fund?

- I read a great story about the company that said now was the time to act.
- My friend told me she made a 100 percent return on a stock, and I asked myself, "Why her?"
- The markets are breaking new highs every other day, and I felt left out.
- I read yet another story about the urgent need to plan for retirement.
- I learned through a seminar that the only way to make money these days is through the stock market.

Which of the following sentences applied to you a few minutes or days before you sold a stock or shares of a mutual fund?

- I read in the paper today that the economy is going to tank, oil prices are going to skyrocket, and consumers will have no money left.
- My friend told me that he now sits on the fence after making a lot of money selling his stocks.
- My stock just dropped another 5 percent on top of the 20 percent it had already lost.
- I read yet another story about the urgent need to plan for retirement.
- I learned through a seminar that the only way to make money these days is to buy gold/silver, purchase a vacation house/second condo, or collect art.

Do any of the above sound familiar? How many times have you asked yourself, "Why did I buy this stock in the first place?" or "Why can't I make money like Joe?"

As humans, we are driven by several psychological factors that may explain why we aren't making the right decisions when it comes to buying and selling stocks. I'll discuss two of them in this chapter.

<u>The first factor—the fear of losing (or losing too much)</u>

Let's say you had to choose between the following two alternatives: a sure gain of $240 and a 25 percent chance of gaining $1,000 with a 75 percent chance of gaining $0. Which one would you choose?

According to statistics, you should choose the second option, in which you would have gained $250.

Now consider these two alternatives: a sure loss of $240 and a 25 percent chance of losing $1,000 with a 75 percent chance of losing $0. Which one would you choose?

Why do we sell low and buy high?

According to statistics, you should choose the first option—a sure loss of $240.

Which option did you choose?

Studies show that people feel the pain of loss twice as much as they feel pleasure from an equal gain. Consider your point of view; would you gain more pleasure from winning $100 or suffer more agony from losing $100? What if the figure were $10,000?

Most investors tend to sell an investment prematurely because they cannot bear to "suffer" any longer. How many times has this happened to you? Even worse, how many times have you sold a stock only to see it rise immediately after? In those cases it is important to keep in mind that the stock doesn't know you. It isn't rising just to upset you. It's all in your head.

So what can be done about this? How about familiarizing yourself with the value of a company **before** you purchase its stock? How about knowing the sell price **before** you buy?

<u>The second factor—the need to be liked and our urgency society</u>

We are conditioned as children to believe that we are who our friends are. We develop personality traits similar to those of our friends and tend to act in ways that we believe will get people to like us and want to be around us. After all, don't we all want to be popular? Who wants to be the kid standing all alone on the playground?

As we get older, we are conditioned to buy into society's urgency mentality. How do you feel when the phone rings? Do you feel a pressing urge to answer it? The media contributes largely to this mentality by using words like "now," "last chance," and "don't miss the bus."

These two psychological factors greatly affect our investment abilities. When our friends share their investment successes, we want to be on their winning team. When we're told, "Be sure not to miss the party," we immediately feel the need to join the party. (Wouldn't it be great to stand around at the Friday party with all your friends and tell stories about your stock market successes?) All of this causes us to believe that the only way to join the party is to do what your friends are doing, in this case buying and selling stocks.

As investors we feel more comfortable with the knowledge that our friends and peers own the same stock as we do. It's interesting to consider that we feel better knowing that if we lose money on a specific stock, we won't be the only ones.

So what can you do about this? There is a third option: **deciding** not to buy a stock is also a choice that we can **act upon**. Regarding the need to feel liked, take a moment to consider your end goal. Is your goal in investing to make friends or to create wealth?

Chapter 2
Why do we sell low and buy high? Part 2

As I mentioned in the last chapter, we are driven throughout our lifetimes by several psychological factors that may explain why we aren't making the right decisions when it comes to buying and selling stocks. In this chapter, I will expand on the need to be liked factor and will introduce two new behavioral factors that affect our decision process—our tendency to be overconfident and our need to comply with our previous commitments.

<u>To be liked or not to be liked: that is the question.</u>

There is a good reason why we are conditioned and almost addicted to the idea of being liked and, furthermore, why we are afraid of not being liked. Remember your school days. Who did you want to be? Did you want to be the kid that was the most popular or the kid no one would speak to? Did you want to come to parties on your own or with other kids? How did you feel about the kid who sat next to the teacher on the annual school trip because no one else wanted to sit next to him or her?

So why do we want to be liked? The simple answer is that life usually works much better for us when we are liked than when we are disliked. As far back as the early days on this planet, humans who got along with and were liked by others generally fared much better than those who weren't liked. In the beginning of time, taking care of each other was a must in order to survive, and who likes to take care of someone they disdain? It's very simple; for most of us, being liked means having more opportunities to have good friends, better work, and happier lives in general. Being liked is a great thing. What's the problem with that?

Consider the following scenario: if you could purchase only one stock, would you be more likely to purchase a stock owned by a group of your friends who recommended it to you or a stock recommended by your next-door neighbor who insists on mowing the lawn when you take a nap? If you chose the second option, what are you planning to tell your friends when they ask about it? Even worse, how will you feel when they brag about the big success they had? There's not an easy answer.

As opposed to the great benefits of being liked as part of your place in society, making an investing decision based on the level of approval you will obtain as a result is not always a smart move. When making an investment decision, we need to ask ourselves some of these questions:

1. What is the value of the company versus its current price?
2. What are the company's future prospects?
3. How effective is the company management?
4. Do I really know enough in order to make a smart decision? If not, where can I learn more?

We tend to like people who provide us with value and knowledge. Answering the above questions and discussing them with your friends will allow you to make savvier investment choices and will increase your popularity because of the valuable knowledge you possess. In the next chapter, we'll discuss these questions and meet the famous Mr. Market created by Professor Benjamin Graham. Stay tuned.

Overconfidence and commitment

Do you think most people are confident in themselves? You might find it interesting to learn the following:

- In a study conducted in Sweden by the University Of Stockholm, subjects were asked about their competence as drivers in relation to a group of drivers. It was found that 88 percent of the participants believed themselves to be safer than the median driver.
- Nineteen percent of Americans believe they are among the richest 1 percent in the world.
- Eighty-one percent of new business owners think their own business has at least a 70 percent chance of success, but only 39 percent think that any business like theirs would be likely to succeed.
- The US Census Bureau reports that 50 percent of new ventures close within the first four years.

How would you answer the questions that were asked in the first three studies above?

Confidence is very important in making any decision, and the lack of it can prevent us from making even simple decisions. However, overconfidence—especially overconfidence that is not backed with key facts—can be fatal to your investment results.

On top of being overconfident, we also tend to commit and even anchor to our previous decisions.

Think about the following questions:

- Would you be willing to buy a stock today that was cheaper six months ago?

- Would you be willing to sell a stock you own that is now priced at half the price per share it reached six months ago?

In a 2004 shareholder meeting, Warren Buffett said, "I bought something at $X, and it went up to $X and 1/8. I sometimes stopped buying, perhaps hoping it would come back down. We've missed billions when I've gotten anchored." The mix of overconfidence in ourselves and our tendency to anchor and commit to our previous decisions can lead to undesirable results.

What can we do to avoid this? The first step is to acknowledge these traits and not allow yourself to be fooled into believing that you are different. As Richard Feynman said, "The first principle is that you must not fool yourself, and you are the easiest person to fool."

Other ways to avoid these psychological factors when investing are:

- **Before** purchasing a stock, write down why you decided to purchase that stock at this price and what factors or changes will motivate you to sell the stock.
- Use checklists to make sure that you have covered (and checked) everything you want to know about a company **before** making a commitment.
- Keep searching for new information, especially information that does not agree with your theories.
- Admit your mistakes.

What should you check before purchasing or selling a stock? How do you know the value of a company? Why does it take longer for people to plan their vacation than to purchase a stock? I'll answer these questions and many more in the next chapter.

Chapter 3
Hello, Mr. Market

In the previous chapters, I described some of our thought processes and mindsets when we buy or sell a stock. I discussed our fear of losing, our craving to be liked, and our need to act immediately. We also saw how overconfidence and commitment to previous decisions or information can impact our investment decision process.

My intention in this chapter is to introduce you to Mr. Market, the manic-depressive figure that was created in the mind of the brilliant professor Benjamin Graham. I will also present a different point of view toward investing in the stock market.

Before we start talking about Mr. Market, let me ask a very simple question: **What is a stock?** Easy question, isn't it? Before reading any further, take thirty seconds to answer it.

Here are some answers I've been given in response to that very question:

- A stock is a sure way to make (or lose) money.
- A stock is a company.
- A stock is the price of a company.
- Stocks are these really annoying three-letter words that run along the bottom of my CNBC screen and make me dizzy.

A stock is a representation of a partial ownership of a business or company. For example, think of a media company. We'll call it MyMediaCompany. The company has one million shares (or stocks) outstanding, which means that by buying one share of MyMedia-Company, you will own one millionth of MyMediaCompany. It is very important to be clear about this concept. A stock is not just a ticker or a three-letter word; a stock represents a partial ownership in a business, which means that as a partial owner of MyMediaCompany you partially own its Website, movie studios, TV channels, book publishing, theme parks, cruise lines, hotels, media stores, etc. You get my point. By owning a stock of MyMediaCompany, you are a partial owner of everything MyMediaCompany owns.

Why is it so important to understand this concept? Let's explore some of the answers that I received to the question, "Why did you buy a stock (or shares) of a company?"

- I bought the stock at $5 because $5 is a cheap price.
- I bought the stock because my friends own it.
- I bought the stock because it used to be $50 and is now $20, so it must be cheap.
- I bought the stock because it has to go up.
- I bought the stock because the yelling news anchor said the price graph is in a head-and-shoulders formation and is reaching the price breaking point. (Yes, someone really told me that!)

All of these answers focus on the one piece of information that is the easiest to get—the stock price. Yet all of these answers ignore the most important question we should ask ourselves: **What is the value of the company behind the ticker,** the company that this stock represents? Only by understanding the **value** of the company can you tell if the price of the stock is cheap or expensive.

Valuing a company is not an easy task, but it is the first and most important step that needs to happen **before** you purchase a stock. Peter Lynch once said, *"Spend at least as much time researching a stock as you would choosing a refrigerator."*

Now that we know that a stock represents a partial ownership of a company and the importance of valuing the company before looking at the price of its stock, it is easy to conclude that only when you know the value of the company and the offering price will you be able to make a prudent investment decision. Warren Buffet tells us, *"Price is what you pay; value is what you get."* Always demand more value for your purchase price.

So who decides the price of the stock? Again, I went out and asked a few people that question. Here are some of the more interesting answers I received:

- The market decides the price.
- The government decides the price.
- The companies decide the price.
- It's all one big gambling machine.
- The ticker decides the price. (Yes, I have heard that.)

There's probably some truth in every answer. The real answer is that in the short term, **we**—the investors (and all sort of other automatic software programs)—decide the market price of a stock. In the long run, **the company's results** impact its market price.

Where is this price being decided? That's an easy question. It's decided in the stock exchange. But what is the stock exchange? For the sake of simplicity, let's think about the stock exchange as a big market in which people decide how much they are willing to pay in order to buy a share of a company and at what price they are willing to sell it.

At last, here comes Mr. Market.

Professor Benjamin Graham, who is known as the dean of value investing and has written two fabulous books that are a must for any serious investor (*Security Analysis* and *The Intelligent Investor*), created a character he called Mr. Market to explain the above concepts. You can think of Mr. Market as a character with one duty—to visit every day and offer to buy or sell a fractional share in a company at whatever price he sees fit. His most useful characteristic is that he will not take any offense if you ignore him; he will still return the next day with another price offer.

If we're investing from a business prospective, we will ignore Mr. Market until our facts (obtained by our own research) indicate that his quoted price has a wide discount from the true value of the business he is trying to sell or buy. We can ignore him in all other cases, knowing he will always show up the next day with another offer. The important question we should ask ourselves is will we let Mr. Market's daily quotation determine the true value of an investment, or will it be **us** who determines the true value and use Mr. Market's manic-depressive behavior to our own advantage by buying from him when he offers stock at a foolishly low price and selling to him when he offers to buy at an equally foolish high price?

It is **you** who decides whether to let Mr. Market influence your investment decisions or to let your research, facts, and reasoning prevail. As Benjamin Graham said, *"Mr. Market is there to serve you, not to guide you. It is his pocketbook, not his wisdom, that you will find useful."*

And what should you do in all the other times? Nothing. Remember, a decision not to buy and not to sell is one of the most important decisions an investor can make. All you need to do is deepen your knowledge and wait for the next time, when you'll be able to take advantage of dear Mr. Market.

Mr. Charles Munger likes to say, *"You don't make money when you buy stocks, and you don't make money when you sell stocks. You make money by waiting."*

Why do we sell low and buy high?

What do you do when you wait? Why do we feel unable to wait? Is waiting really that simple? I will answer these questions and many more in the next chapter.

Chapter 4
Let's go shopping, Part 1

In the previous chapter, I explained the meaning of a stock; the most important fact to remember is that a stock represents a partial ownership of a company. Then we discussed the stock exchange, the big market in which people decide how much they're willing to pay in order to buy a share of a company and at what price they're willing to sell it. Lastly I wrote about Mr. Market, the manic-depressive figure that was conceived in the mind of Professor Benjamin Graham.

My intention in this chapter is to introduce you to a better way of shopping for stocks and explain what to do before you go shopping. It might sound surprising, but the real work happens **before** you purchase your partial ownership in a company.

But before we go shopping for stocks, let's start with a simple question. Why do businesses sell their products or services?

That's easy, right? Most businesses sell their products or services in order to make money. It's quite a simple idea. If I sell to you for $10 a product that cost me $5, I will make a profit of $5. That is also the reason why businesses want to sell more and more; if I sell you two products for $10 each that cost me $5 each, I will earn an even greater profit.

Now that we know why businesses sell their products or services, we must ask a bigger question, one which might sound trivial but holds a lot of importance to us: why do companies sell their stocks on the stock exchange every day?

You might think they do it for the same reason they sell their products; if they sell their stocks, they'll earn more money. It makes sense, right? Well, unfortunately the answer is no. In most cases the companies are **not** the ones that sell you their stocks.* Wait a second, you say. Did you just tell me the companies are not the ones who sell the stocks? Yes, usually the companies themselves do not sell stocks on the stock market for you to buy.

You may be a bit puzzled. If the company doesn't sell its stocks, who does? We do—the investors of the world. It might be a person sitting in his home selling shares of a single company or mutual fund managers selling shares of thousands of companies. It might be a pension fund selling shares of companies or banks with partial ownership in companies selling some of their shares. It might even be employees of the company that sell their own company shares.

You see, for every person that buys shares, there is another person that sells them. Interesting, right? **For every buyer, there is a seller, and for every seller, there is a buyer.** Most of the time, the buyer and the seller think they are making the correct decision while the other person is wrong.

Let's take thirty seconds and ask ourselves how many times we make a decision knowing it is the wrong one. Hopefully it doesn't happen too many times for most of us; otherwise we'd have a lot of explaining to do. We tend to make decisions based on the assumption that we're making the right decision, and yet in the stock market almost every transaction has two sides and two people, each making the opposite decision and each believing they're making the right one.

* *There is, of course, a caveat to that statement. The first time a company "goes public." the company itself issues its stocks in the market.*

Why do we sell low and buy high?

So how do you know you're the one who made the right decision? As the saying goes, "If you're in a poker game for thirty minutes and you don't know who the patsy is, you are the patsy." How do we make sure that at the stock market table we aren't the patsy?

Before we answer that question, let's remember, as we discovered in my previous chapters, that many times people don't make decisions based exclusively on logic and reasoning. As we mentioned, most people rely on the one piece of information that is the easiest to get—the stock price—and ignore the most important question we should ask: what is the **value** of the company behind the ticker, the company that this stock represents?

Rule number one to keep from being the patsy is to do what other people are not doing. We need to separate the value of the business from the market price. Mr. Market represents decisions of the people. We need to come up with our **own** decisions that value the company based on facts and reasoning, and only then should we decide whether to take advantage of Mr. Market's decisions. As Benjamin Graham said, *"Mr. Market is there to serve you, not to guide you. It is his pocketbook, not his wisdom, that you will find useful."*

How do we go about doing that? How do we know the value of a company?

Think about the following questions: What is the value of a company? What is the value of any assets you may have?

Let's assume you own a rental apartment. What is the value of this asset? Here are some answers I have received to that question:

- It's worth the price you receive when you sell the apartment.
- It's worth the amount of rent you can collect **and** the selling price of the apartment.
- It's worth nothing if you don't have renters.

17

- My head is spinning already with all these questions. Why can't you just tell me the answer?

Many great investors have said that the intrinsic value of a company is **the discounted value of the cash that can be taken out of a business during its remaining life.** Those are big words indeed. Let's try to simplify it. Going back to the rental apartment, what is the cash that we can take out of our rental property? In other words, how much is left for me?

The net cash from the rental property will be the money we receive from rental fees after subtracting all maintenance expenses (such as painting, fixing broken items, and all the things we handy people love to do), mortgage payments, interest expenses, insurance costs, taxes, and any other services we might need.

Assuming we can rent our apartment for $1,000 a month, and if our expenses on average are $800 a month, then our net cash will be $200 a month. That makes sense, right? $200 a month is the cash we can expect to get from the apartment during its remaining life. If we know we're going to hold the apartment for 10 years, we can expect to get $24,000 in cash after all expenses.

Some of you might ask, "What about the purchase price? What about the selling price? What about increases in rent fees? What about increases in maintenance costs?" These are all excellent questions.

The definition of intrinsic value is simple; however, calculating it is not easy. I'll go into much more detail about assumptions and other items to consider when calculating the value of an asset (or a company) in the next chapter, but for now, I think we're ready for rule number two to keep us from being the patsy: calculating intrinsic value will enable us to pay the right price for a company. Remember, valuing a company is part science and part art. There is no one intrinsic value. It will usually be a range. *It is better to be roughly right than precisely wrong.*

Some of you might ask, "What do we need to look at in order to calculate the intrinsic value of a company? What do we need to check in order to figure out the cash that will stay in the company's pocket and in our pockets, as partial owners?"

Chapter 5
Let's go shopping, Part 2

In the previous chapter, I started to discuss the process of purchasing stocks, who the buyers and sellers in the stock market are, and the importance of separating a stock price from the value of a company when making an investment decision. I also talked about the important concept of intrinsic value—the discounted value of the cash that can be taken out of a business during its remaining life.

My intention in this chapter is to introduce you to the three key aspects in evaluating a company and suggest a more intelligent way of shopping for stocks. I will also expand on the concept of intrinsic value.

Let's begin by taking thirty seconds to think about how we find the right university for our kids. I know for some people this question may cause a mild anxiety attack, but I've put together a list of the key questions that help us make the right decision in this area:

- Does the university offer the subjects that my child wants to learn? (After all, at the end of the day it's their decision, not ours.)
- Does the university offer the services my child will need?
- What is the university's reputation among current students?
- How strong is the alumni group?
- What do we know about the teachers?
- What are the counselors like?
- How good is the dean?

- How much will it cost to send my child to this university?
- Does the university provide grants? Loans? What are the terms?
- Will a degree in this field from this particular university increase my child's earning potential over a degree from a different university?

If you had to arrange the above questions into three groups, how would you do it? Take a few minutes to think about it.

The three key questions we're trying to answer are:

- What is the quality of the **university**?
- What is the quality of the **people** who work for the university?
- What are the **financials** behind acquiring a degree from this university, and what will be the financial benefits as a result of acquiring the degree at this university?

Get yourself a brownie if, after reading the last question, you jumped up and shouted, "This is like asking the difference between price and value."

Some of you might be thinking, this is really helpful, but what does it have to do with shopping for stocks? Excellent question! The answer is that the same key areas we focus on when choosing a university can be applied to purchasing stocks, and these key questions should be answered **before** purchasing shares of a company in the stock market, and no, "Do I trust my friend's tips?" is not one of them. I find it quite puzzling that some people don't agree that key questions should be answered **prior** to the purchase of the company.

Why do we sell low and buy high?

When shopping for companies to invest in, we need to focus on these three key areas:

- The company
- The people
- The financials (the difference between the intrinsic value of the business and the price offered to us by Mr. Market, as discussed in my previous chapters)

In the previous chapter, I discussed the value of an asset and the definition of intrinsic value, which is the cash we can take out of a business during its remaining business life. I emphasized that estimating the intrinsic value of a company and purchasing its stocks below their intrinsic value is a key aspect of a successful investment. However, **all three areas** needed to be explored in order to estimate the company's intrinsic value.

I have often found that people believe all you need to know in order to calculate a company's intrinsic value are its financials. Some of the reasons people have given for this belief are:

- If I know the cash that the business generated in the past five years, why do I need to learn anything else?
- What does it matter who runs the business? What matters is the financials. CEOs come and go. The company is what stays.
- Learning about an organization is a waste of time. Let me just turn on the TV, see the list of hot stocks, and join the party.

What do *you* think? Is it enough to look at the financials of a business? Even worse, is checking a stock price on the Internet enough to learn about its value and make an investment decision? I hope you already know better.

I believe this is a key mistake for many investors. You **cannot** estimate the value of a company without **understanding** the company and its leaders. We'll talk more about the leaders in the next chapter. Let's focus now on the importance of understanding the company itself.

Why is it important to know a company in which you're considering investing? Let's go back to our example of the rental unit. Assuming you own a rental unit, we asked, what is the **value** of this asset?

If we consider only the financials of the rental unit, all we may know is that in the past five years it generated an average of $250,000 in rental fees, maintenance costs were $100,000, and all other expenses (legal fees, taxes, etc.) cost another $100,000. In that case, the owner of the rental unit generated an average of $50,000 a year.

Rental Income: $250,000
- Expenses: $200,000
_____

Net Cash: $ 50,000

If this is all we know, we can easily fool ourselves and say, "If I can buy this business at a price below $200,000, and if the income and expenses continue to be what they have been for the past five years, it's a great deal." Remember, the business generates $50,000 for you each year, so in five years it will generate $250,000.

But wait a second. Let's ask ourselves the following questions:

- Would we be happy if we knew that on similar units the yearly maintenance cost is $150,000 instead of $100,000?

- What would happen if we knew that a new apartment building will be constructed next to our unit in the next two years and that it is rumored that the rent fees for the new apartments will be lower than ours, with much better amenities?
- Would we pay the same price if the apartment is in New York, Detroit, or Ghana?
- What would happen if we knew the occupancy rate of our apartment was 100 percent in the past five years because it was occupied by only one tenant, who is now retiring and planning to move to Florida?
- What would happen if we knew that new regulations are going to impact apartment owners?

Knowing nothing about the business except its financials is similar to a one-legged man competing in an ass-kicking tournament; you might stay on your feet for a while, but you won't win.

What are the important questions we need to ask ourselves about a company **prior** to purchasing its shares? What do we want to know in order to be comfortable in estimating its intrinsic value? Is it possible to value any company regardless of its industry and characteristics? Do we know the organization we have purchased?

I'll discuss these questions in the next chapter, but before I finish this chapter, I want to challenge the brave readers out there to look at your decision-making process from the opposite side, following the German mathematician Carl Gustav Jacobi's maxim, "Invert, always invert." Take ten minutes and ask yourself what key questions will probably **not** help you make the right decision when choosing a university for your child. Light bulb! What questions will not give insights when deciding whether or not to buy shares of a company? What noise do you need to ignore?

Chapter 6
This is the world we live in

In the previous chapter, I began to discuss the three key aspects of evaluating an investment—understanding the company, evaluating its leaders, and deciphering its financials to determine its intrinsic value. I focused on the first aspect, understanding the company, and briefly mentioned why understanding only the financials of an organization is not enough to evaluate a business when determining whether to purchase its stocks.

My intention in this chapter is to continue on the subject of the importance of understanding a company and to raise some of the questions to ask **prior** to investing in a company or purchasing its stocks. I want to emphasize again that in order to be an intelligent investor, **all three aspects** need to be explored in order to estimate the intrinsic value of a company.

What type of companies do you understand? Can you understand all types? Can you understand only one? How will you know?

For those of you who think you can understand any type of company, take a few minutes to think about these questions:

- Do you know how organizations in the oil and exploration industry make money? What is the cost of operating a rig? What is the amount of money a company must earn per barrel of oil to be profitable? What is the cost of insuring operations? What is the future of the oil reserves?

- In the media industry, do you know the cost of creating an animation movie? What is the cost of marketing and distributing a movie? What is and will be the impact of the Internet on cable TV and on the industry? What is the cost per client of maintaining a cable infrastructure? What is the impact of people "cutting the line?" Can you predict whether or not a movie will be successful? What is the importance of a brand? Will a child prefer to watch one channel over another because of a brand? What is the future of music? Books? Newspapers?
- In the chocolate and candy industry, do you know how a 10 percent change in the price of a pound of Brazilian cocoa will impact the price of chocolates in a store? What about a 10 percent change in the price of a pound of sugar? Do people consume more chocolate in the winter or in the summer? Do people purchase more chocolate in supermarkets or in drug stores? Does it matter? How is the trend toward eating healthy foods affecting the chocolate industry? What is the pricing power of a chocolate manufacturer? And a tricky question: what is the number one holiday for chocolate sales in the United States? (I'll give you a hint; it isn't Valentine's Day.)
- In the retail industry, is it better to own a store or lease it? What is the difference in cost between operating a store in an "A" type mall and a "C" type mall? What is the difference in cost between manufacturing in China and Mexico? What is the inventory turnover of your favorite retailer? (Some of you are starting to make faces at me. Yes, I see you!)

Do you still think you can understand any industry and any business? We haven't even mentioned property/casualty insurance, the auto industry, the software industry, or the telecomm industry.

Why do we sell low and buy high?

The important point we must take from all these questions is not our ability to answer them but our ability to distinguish which industries we are more familiar with and, furthermore, our ability to ask the right questions. We can't ask questions about industries we don't understand, and if we don't **understand** an industry or company, how can we **value** it?

I'll give you two minutes to think about that last question, but for those who want to move ahead, the answer is *we can't!* If we don't understand it, we cannot value it. The first question to ask when evaluating a possible investment is, "Do I understand it?" If the answer is no, go on to the next investment opportunity.

To summarize, the first important aspect of understanding a business is to draw what Warren Buffett calls our circle of competence—the area in which we excel, the businesses we can understand better than other people, the place in which we have a competitive advantage. As Tom Watson said, *"I'm no genius, but I'm smart in spots, and I stay around those spots."*

I hope you are now convinced to first explore the companies in your circle of competence. It is important to remember that it is not the *size* of your area of understanding that will define your success; knowing its *boundaries* will define your investment success.

By now you are probably asking, "How do I know what my circle of competence is, and how do I expand it?"

I believe that your first area of competency is your profession, or the industry you work in. For example, if you work in the hospitality industry, you will know more than other people about occupancy rates, rates per room, trends in the industry, and management operations. I suggest you start looking for potential investments by researching hospitality companies. If you work in the retail industry, you might know more than other people about inventory, fashion trends, brand names, distribution networks, and operating a retail store. You might want to start your search with retail companies. If you work for a software company, you might know more than other people about costs of research and development, the software development life cycle, software products marketing, and the cost of acquiring new technologies.

You get my point. What you do most of your workday is probably the current center of your circle of knowledge, and it's a good place from which to start exploring companies.

Let's explore the next question: how do we expand our circle of competence? I believe the best way is to find what are you curious about and what you would like to learn more about.

In real estate the three keys to success are location, location, and location. To expand your circle of knowledge, the three keys to success are reading, listening, and thinking. Read about the industry you're interested in and the companies within it. Listen to people from the industry and come up with your own questions to gain deeper understanding about the industry. This is a long process. Learning is an ongoing journey; enjoy it and remember how to separate the important knowledge from the noise.

Let's continue discovering how to understand a company. What areas should we focus on when trying to understand an organization? Before I highlight some of these areas, here are some questions people usually ask when evaluating a company:

- How will sales grow ten years from now?
- How much market share will the company acquire in the next five years?
- How can the company defeat its competitors?

Why do we sell low and buy high?

- What are the company's competitive advantages?

Let's go back to the German mathematician Carl Gustav Jacobi and his maxim, "Invert, always invert." How can we ask the above questions differently? Maybe something like this:

- What could decrease company sales in the next ten years?
- How can the company's competitors gain market share from the company?
- What could cause the company to fail?
- What are the *perceived* competitive advantages? What would happen if these disappear?

Interesting, right? As we discussed before, sometimes asking the questions in a different way can lead us to discover important information that will help us make a knowledgeable decision. Do not limit yourself to the obvious questions; invert, always invert.

In the next chapter, I will continue to drill down into more specific areas that will help us understand a company, but before I finish this chapter, let's take a look at confirmation bias and the art of asking the right questions.

Confirmation bias is our tendency to favor information that confirms our existing perceptions, regardless of whether the information is true. As a result we gather (or retrieve from memory) evidence that confirms our perceptions and interpret that evidence in a biased way. Because of this tendency, our ability to ask questions is crucial to avoid confirmation basis when evaluating a possible investment.

Let me conclude with a process that may help you. Think about your greatest current investment idea. Which investment was a "sure thing?" Which investment were you most excited about? Next time you get excited about a specific investment or company, try to find at least three reasons why **not** to invest in that business. Killing your best ideas before others do so is a key to successful investment.

Much more about understanding a company, the areas to question, and how to kill ideas is coming up in the next chapter.

Chapter 7
Money, money, money

In the previous chapter, I explored the first of the three aspects of evaluating an investment—understanding the company itself. I explained the importance of knowing your circle of competence, how to define it, and how to expand it. I concluded the chapter with a discussion about confirmation bias.

My intention in this chapter is to delve deeper into the importance of understanding a company before investing in it and to offer more specific details about the aspects of a company we should question. Keep in mind that these questions (and hopefully their answers) should be dealt with **prior** to investing in any company or purchasing its stocks.

As mentioned in the previous chapter, the first question to ask when considering investing in a company is whether we can understand the company. How do you know that, you ask? I believe that by asking yourself three questions and performing a simple exercise, you will be comfortable enough to investigate further. The three questions are:

1. How does the company generate money?
2. How will the company generate money five or ten years from today?
3. What could destroy the company?

Think about a few companies in which you are interested and write down answers to the above questions for each one. Which was the toughest question to answer?

The simple exercise (suggested by the legendary investor Peter Lynch) is this: stand in front of a mirror and talk for five minutes about why you might want to invest in each of the companies in which you are interested. Start by saying, "I want to invest in Company X because..." and continue with, "I think Business X is a great investment because..."

Great! Now that you feel the business you're investigating is within your circle of competence, let's think about the strategic areas to explore within the company. Your goal should be to gather substantial knowledge about the company in order to prevent yourself from succumbing to confirmation bias.

Charles Munger often talks about the value of effective checklists to minimize errors and omissions. Are you ready to create our first checklist? (This is not a trick question. The answer is yes.)

Competitive advantages

The first items on our checklist will be geared toward exploring what I like to call the moats around a company—its advantages over its competitors. Here are some of the questions you should ask regarding the competitive advantage of an organization:

- Does the company have pricing power? In other words, can it increase the prices of its products and services without losing massive amounts of its clients?
- What are the switching costs? In other words, what costs will a client incur when switching from this company to another?

- For a customer oriented business, how are the products and/or services integrated into the client's day-to-day life (habits)?
- For a business-to-business company, how are the products and/or services integrated into the purchasing business's day-to-day operations?
- If you had $100 million, could you build a competing business?
  - o Could you replicate the business's distribution system?
  - o Does the company have long-term patents, copyrights, or other intellectual property?
  - o Does the company require any specific resources to which others do not have access?
- How strong is the company brand name? Try to answer this question from pricing power and habit/behavioral points of view.
- Does the company dominate any specific local or regional niche?
- Is the organization a monopoly or duopoly in an unregulated industry?
- Is the business required to comply with specific and complex government regulations?

Let's take a closer look at the first two questions on our checklist.

Pricing Power. Do you think pricing power (the ability of a business to increase the price of its products without losing clients) is important? If you don't think so, try comparing a business that can easily increase its prices with one that would lose customers with any single increase in its prices. What is the difference between these two businesses? Which one would you like to own?

One of the reasons that pricing power is such a crucial aspect of a business is the effect of inflation, which is also known as the hidden tax. For example, if you earn a $100,000 salary today at a very low 2 percent inflation and without the ability to increase your salary, your purchasing power (The value of money, as measured by the quantity and quality of products and services it can buy) will be about $67,000 in twenty years. I don't mean to depress you, but at the United States' inflation rate of 3.42 percent (1913-2007), a $100,000 salary will give you after twenty years a purchasing power of only about $50,000.

A business that cannot raise its prices without losing a significant number of its clients will face the same issue. Let me give you an example. Let's say you're investigating a business that is creating some sort of widget (don't you just love that word?). If this business can never raise the prices of its widgets, then its profits will soon begin to decline, slowly but surely. Why?

The reason for the falling profits is the fact that in the process of manufacturing and selling widgets, the company incurs expenses, such as raw materials needed to create the widgets, rent of a factory or warehouse, salaries for the employees who make the widgets, marketing and sales costs, etc. These expenses will steadily increase over time and cost the business more money, which means that the cost of producing a widget will increase, although the selling price of the widget will not. Therefore the business will make less and less money, until finally it will **lose** money every time it produces a widget. It's not a fairytale ending.

My more advanced readers (yes, that's you) may be thinking that the solution is to gain higher efficiency and productivity and, by doing so, maintain the profit margins. Unfortunately, without the ability to increase the selling price of the widgets, there is a limit to these strategies unless more money is invested in the business.

You can see why pricing power is an important competitive advantage. When researching investment possibilities, we should look for businesses with pricing power and generally avoid the ones without it.

Switching costs. Switching costs represent the costs a client will incur when switching from one business provider to another provider of the same services and/or products. As investors, we should be looking for companies with high switching costs.

As an example, let's think about a decision that does not incur much switching cost. Think of the last time you went to the movie theatre. You were standing with your kids, looking at the list of movies playing. There were three kids' movies. One of your children wanted to see *Bikes 2*, while the other two wanted to see a different movie. Two minutes of arguing and a boxful of popcorn later, you all decided to go to the other movie. The switching costs of making the decision of which movie to see were very low, and because of that, the company that produced *Bikes 2* lost several clients.

Can you name a few businesses with high switching costs? What is unique about each of these businesses? I will leave these questions for you to explore on your own, but let me give you some hints. Think of a business whose services are completely integrated into the day-to-day operations of its customers. Switching from this business's services will require its users to go through extensive training and might result in significant disruption. Do you know of any business like that?

Now we know that we need to research and learn more about the competitive advantages of a company prior to investing in it. You may want to write down the competitive advantages checklist and use it when researching investment opportunities.

As mentioned before, let's not forget how to overcome our confirmation bias. If we find a business with competitive advantages that has built over the years a wide and deep moat filled with piranhas and crocodiles, we can feel very good about that business, and at that point we should start compiling more information to confirm our great find.

Stop!

Now it is time to look for information that will kill our theory—information that might help us see the company from a different angle. Here are some questions that you might want to ask yourself:

- What technology, industry trends, or regulatory changes could kill the competitive advantage of the company?
- Could an influential person with $10 million create a competing business? If not, why not? Could they do it with $1 billion?
- Is there a competitive replacement product or service that would enable a current client to receive the same benefits elsewhere at a lower cost?
- What could prevent the business from growing? What could kill the industry in which the organization operates?

Can you think of any other questions to add to the list?

We've covered a lot of information about understanding a business, and we'll cover even more in the next chapter, as well as the human aspects of a business.

I would like to share a question someone posed to me not long ago after I had explained to him the process of understanding a business. He said, "This process of discovery will take a lot of time, and there aren't many businesses that will fit these criteria. I might end up with owning just few businesses. Isn't that the opposite of the investment idea of wide diversification?" Good question. Think about it. What are you trying to achieve with diversification? How does it fit into your overall investing goals?

We'll be able to answer this question after completing our tool set in the next chapter and then exploring the next two aspects of evaluating an investment, people and financials.

Chapter 8
The business network and customer habits

In the previous chapter, I continued my discussion of the first of the three aspects of evaluating an investment—understanding the company. I advised the use of checklists to explore the moats around a business and explained the value of a company's pricing power and client switching costs. I concluded the chapter with a defense against confirmation bias—looking for anything that could kill any positive trait of a company that seems to be a good investment.

My intention in this chapter is to finish our discussion about understanding an organization and to offer more insights into the key information we need to gather prior to investing in a company.

In the previous chapter, I listed important competitive advantages to explore when evaluating an investment. In this chapter I'll discuss two more competitive advantages: the network effect and customer captivity.

Let's start with the network effect. What is the network effect? In business, it's what happens when the number of users (or customers) increases the value of a company. I know that sounds a bit confusing, so an example is in order.

In the old days (before the Internet and all sorts of berries), newspapers used to create a network effect; the more people read the same newspaper, the more the value of that paper's classified ads increased, and the value of the paper to all of its subscribers increased, as well. So the number of readers (the network) of the newspaper gave it its value, even though the readers didn't intend to create value for other readers by subscribing to the newspaper.

Of course, we can see immediately how the network effect can be a competitive advantage for an organization. When a successful company reaches a certain volume of users, each additional user will increase the value of the company.

What are some companies that make use of the network effect? You can discover some of these companies by asking yourself the following questions:

- What social network do you use on a daily basis? Why do you use it?
- Who is your cable provider?
- On which stock exchange are high-profile companies being traded?
- Where did you post your ad to sell that old sofa?
- How many commercial railroad companies are in the United States?

Think about the volume of the companies' user bases when answering the above questions. Do the user bases create a network effect? Who will benefit from an increase in the number of users? (Answer: the company.)

Companies who have successfully made use of network effect will usually have better economics than other companies.

When evaluating a company's network effect, ask the following questions:

- What could erode the network effect of a company? (Think newspapers.)
- Could government regulations impact the network effect?
- Does a niche business have a stronger network effect then a global one?
- Will the network effect of your researched company exist ten or twenty years from now? What will sustain it? What could destroy it?

This leads us to the second competitive advantage that a good company will have: customer captivity. In the previous chapter I introduced one aspect of customer captivity—switching costs; the higher the cost for a user to switch from one service (or product) to another, the higher that company's user captivity is. Now let's discuss another aspect of customer captivity—habit.

Companies that can create an "addiction" to their product by encouraging consistently high frequency of use of its products or services can create a habit of consumption of their product. These companies will have greater costumer captivity and a competitive advantage over companies that have to convince their customer to buy their product every single time instead of just the first time. As an added bonus, companies with habits of consumption will have greater pricing power, as well.

Think about some of the products you are using on a daily basis.

- Where do you get your coffee on your way to work? What type of coffee do you drink?
- Why do you think daily soap operas TV shows are daily?
- What is the first Website you visit each morning?
- What brand of soda and orange juice do your kids drink?

How do companies increase their customers' habit? Let's look back at the psychological factors that impact our decision process. Especially when we aren't sure what is the right behavior or decision, our tendency is to assume the people around us possess more knowledge about the situation than we do, and we think following their decision will make the most sense. Sometimes this tendency is referred to as "social proof."

Think about your favorite soda commercial. Remember the great 1970s Coca Cola commercial? How many people were in that commercial? There were many people, and they all drank the same drink. Think about your favorite fast food commercial. Yes, it will show the food, but usually it will show people just like you (or people like you want to be) all doing the same activity—consuming the product and enjoying it.

Let's look at another example. How do you buy music? Have you ever seen any commercial that influenced you to buy it that way? What was in the commercial? People, many people...

Think again about the two competitive advantages we just talked about—network effect and customer captivity. A company with both of these advantages would have an immense value. More people will consume its products or use its services (customer captivity), and by doing that, they will increase its value (the network effect). Does the company you're researching have these qualities?

As we conclude our discussion about the first aspect of evaluating an investment, I will leave you with the following questions to ask **prior** to investing in a company:

- Is the company a predictable one? How will it look like in the next ten or twenty years? You will find that it is difficult to evaluate a company that changes frequently.

- Is it a simple company? Remember your circle of competence. Do you understand the company? If you do not understand a company, do not even try to evaluate it.

In the last few chapters, we have covered a lot about understanding a business and its competitive advantages. In the next chapter we will move ahead to the next aspect of evaluating a business—the people.

Chapter 9
Looking out for a leader

In the previous chapter, I concluded our discussion about the first of the three aspects of evaluating an investment, understanding the business. I also discussed two competitive advantages—the network effect and customer captivity—and how companies use these to increase their competitive advantage.

My intention in this chapter is to discuss the importance of a company's leaders and the key personal characteristics that they must possess, and to give you a checklist of questions and information that you should look for when evaluating the leaders of a potential investment company.

What do you know about the managers of the company? How do you evaluate the quality of the manager? How do you know the manager's interests align with yours? Who do you think defines and protects the vision and values of the company? Are people more important than process? Does all this really matter when evaluating an investment?

Let's start with the last question. I believe it is extremely important to know and evaluate the manager of the business. Some of you are wondering, "If the company has all the competitive advantages, why does it matter who is running it?"

Think about your favorite soda drink. What happens if the manager of the company who produces it decides to change the formula? (Oh, that rings a bell, think about 1985 new coke) What happens if the manager of an insurance company that insures only safe drivers decides to charge the same premium for not-so-safe drivers? (Did that ever happen?) What happens if the manager of a financial firm believes that house values always increase and bases his or her decisions on this false idea?

It is true that a strong organization can sustain an inadequate manager for a longer period of time than a weak organization, but even a strong company can and will lose its competitive advantages when the wrong manager is at the helm.

How do you know if the manager of the company you want to invest in is the right person? Even more important, how do we go about looking for a leader?

Warren Buffett once mentioned that he looks for three qualities when hiring his managers: personal integrity, intelligence, and a high energy level. He went on to say that if a manager does not have the first quality, the other two will not matter.

Why is integrity so important? It's a silly question, right? Or is it? The definition of integrity based on Random House Dictionary is "adherence to moral and ethical principles; soundness of moral character; honesty."

I think all of us will agree that being an honest person with sound moral character is an important trait for any person, and it is definitely important for a leader of a company we wish to invest in. Who would you rather have as your friend—an honest person or a dishonest person? But why, you might ask, is it so important that the leader of a company is honest? After all, a company leader isn't going to be our friend. We barely even know the person's name, not to mention what he or she looks like. Why not just focus on the financials?

Why do we sell low and buy high?

I know people who hold the firm belief that the only way for a person to become successful and wealthy is to act in their own interest, to be dishonest, and to play in the gray areas with actions more dubious than ethical. It would be easy to dismiss such thoughts as coming from bitter, unsuccessful people who envy successful people. Should we care that the leader is an honest person, or do we want him to do whatever it takes to grow the company, squash the competitors, and achieve the title of the most fearsome person in business?

So here we are. On one hand we want our friends to be moral and honest, and we believe that being an honest person is an important trait. On the other hand, there are people who believe that successful people and leaders of companies need to be sometimes dishonest in order to achieve success.

Here is my take on this dilemma. I think most people are honest and moral, regardless of whether they are our friends, leaders, or the owners of successful companies. I think it is important to associate yourself with people with integrity. It is also important to have integrity yourself, because at the end of the day, people like to do business and work with people they like and respect. As long as you consider yourself an ethical person, why would you want to work for or invest with unethical people? If you do not like to do business with unethical people, neither will others, and companies need to do business with their customers and other companies in order to survive and grow.

If you agree with me, the next questions we need to ask ourselves are how we can tell if a leader has integrity and what makes some leaders act in a dishonest or immoral way.

In order to answer this, let's revisit one of the tendencies I described earlier. We tend to assume the people around us possess more knowledge about the situation then we do and that following their decisions will make the most sense. Most people formulate the definition of a moral or immoral action by looking at what other people are doing. Gray areas become white or black in someone's mind as he or she finds people who fit the behavior for which he or she is searching.

We may quickly come to the conclusion that if a business and its leaders are operating within a less moral environment where immoral actions are allowed, it will be easier for them to justify their less moral actions. This becomes a cycle; as the lines separating moral from immoral conduct become less clear, it becomes easier to not act morally.

Another important point to consider is that our actions are usually driven by the incentives we receive and the consequences we may incur. Let's say you want to invest in a financial services company. When reading the company proxy filing (more about this later), you discover that the company leader's bonuses are based on the company's revenue. You know that in order to get more revenue, the company needs to sell more risky products and/or services to people who do not have the tools to understand the risk. On the other hand, you also discover that the previous leader of the company was fired due to his inability to sell the more conservative products. The new leader sees all the other leaders in the industry acting in a certain way, selling the risky products and making a lot of money for themselves and their companies. The previous leader cannot find a job and was labeled as a person who lost his touch with the new market.

What do you think the current leader of the company will do? If you think he will do exactly what all the others in the industry are doing, you are correct. He will follow the herd and will be compensated to do it, which will only reinforce the behavior.

Why do we sell low and buy high?

What will you do in this situation? There isn't an easy answer. Why should we care about this? The leaders are making the "right" business decisions based on their incentives. What's wrong with that? People are not born immoral; most people follow the herd to justify their behavior and align it with their incentives, losing integrity on the way.

If we agree that having integrity is better than not having it, that we want to surround ourselves with moral people, and that in the long run people like to do business with honorable and likable people, then the big question will be how can we make sure the leader of a potential investment company has integrity?

Our first checklist in this chapter is to be used for evaluating the leaders of an organization, and it begins with one simple question: Do you believe that the business environment promotes immoral behavior? Are the company and its leaders involved in questionable actions? If the answer is yes, then it is more than likely that the leader will not be able to resist the temptation and will act in the same ways as others in the environment.

The next thing you should research is the executive's compensation. Any publicly traded company is obligated to file an annual proxy filing with the Securities and Exchange Commission. You can find these filings by visiting Sec.gov and searching for the company you are investigating (the address for the search page is http://www.sec.gov/edgar/searchedgar/companysearch.html).

In a company's proxy filing (document code DEF 14A), you will find information about the company, such as:

- The director's compensation, election procedures, background, past experiences, and more

- Related person transactions (A related person is any person who is an executive officer, director, a major owner of the company shares or their immediate family members)
- Annual meeting information
- Ownership of common shares (this is where you can find out who else owns shares of the company)

For now, we're primarily interested in the section that describes a leader's compensation, objectives, and philosophy and the company's key people compensation table.

Here are additional questions regarding company leader incentives that I make sure to find answers to before investing:

- Has the company's compensation philosophy changed in the past five or ten years? If so, what were the reasons for the change? Will the reasons benefit the company, its shareholders, or its leader?
- Does the company clearly define the goals to which compensation of its leaders are tied?
- Have the goals changed in bad years to make sure the manager will achieve them? Has the company lowered the bar in bad years? (Yes, it does happen!)
- Are there any other "soft" benefits that the leader receives, such as flying family members on company planes, a golden parachute if the leader is fired, club membership, cars, etc.?

One more key item to research is how many stock shares were **purchased** by the leader as opposed to how many shares were **given** to the leader.

We've covered quite a bit about the desirable traits of company leaders in this chapter. In the next chapter I will add to our checklist for evaluating the leader of a company and will begin to look at the third aspect that we need to explore when evaluating a company—its financials.

Chapter 10
The marathon leader

In the previous chapter, I discussed the second of the three aspects of evaluating an investment—its leaders. I emphasized the importance of acquiring shares in companies that are led by honest and intelligent leaders, and I highlighted some key aspects of the company's proxy filing that will enable you to better evaluate its leaders and their background, incentives, and ownership of the business. My intention in this chapter is to conclude our discussion about the leaders of companies.

How would you operate in your own job if you knew that every three days you had to report your activities to your boss? Would you focus on yearly goals or would you focus on monthly goals, doing a lot in the next three days so your boss will be happy? What would happen if you were given long-term goals and had to report your achievements to your boss every three years?

In the big world of publicly traded companies, most organizations need to report their financials every quarter to their "bosses," who are the shareholders, the directors, and, in the mind of many company leaders, the analysts that cover the company.

Every quarter company leaders make a one-hour conference call to Wall Street analysts who ask them many questions and to whom they explain their company's financial performance and its operation results. The company leaders also have to tell "the world" what they are going to do in the next quarter and what the company's expected financial results will be in the next quarter.

One scenario that is always in the back of the mind of some company leaders is that if the company will miss the goals set in the previous quarter, the company stock price will drop, the analyst will ask tough questions, and the owners will not be happy, which may even result in the leaders looking for a new job. Furthermore, the analyst who covers the company often has his or her own expectations about the company results. Do you think the company leaders want to disappoint their boss?

Would you be able to focus on long-term goals (the ones we would like a company leader to strive toward) if you needed to meet expectations every three months? What would you do if you were the leader of the company? Is it a catch-22 situation or a no-win situation? If you focus on short-term results, you might satisfy your bosses but miss the opportunity for long-term success, which is your true goal. On the other hand, if you focus on long-term goals, your company might benefit but you might miss some of the short-term expectations and may likely get fired before you achieve the long-term goals.

What would you do?

This situation reminds me of a phrase I learned in childhood: *a wise man knows how to **avoid** the peril that a smart man knows how to **get out** of.*

Our focus as investors is to find the leaders who are more like the wise man—the leaders who can **avoid** being cornered in this trap of short-term thinking and activities. We should look for leaders who focus on long-term goals of increasing the company's competitive advantage, increasing the company's value, and creating a long-term culture that is based on long goal setting and tracking while not neglecting the day to day operations within the company.

Why do we sell low and buy high?

How do we find these leaders? Let's go back to incentives. The short-term, "trapped" leaders are the ones who have to focus on the short term; otherwise they might lose their job, disappoint the other shareholders, cause the stock price to drop (temporarily), or all of the above. However, ask yourself this question: what happens if the leader is the largest or a major shareholder of the company? What happens if you know that long-term results are what will define the value of the company and increase its ownership value?

Most leaders know that focusing on the long term is the right thing to do, but most of them cannot do that.

This leads us to our conclusion—aligning ourselves with a major shareholder leader (again, we would like a person who **purchased** shares, not **received** them in forms such as stock options) can be a great benefit to us as investors. There is often (although not always) a better chance that such a leader will focus on the long-term goals of the company to maximize the value of the company, and in so doing maximize his or her own ownership value. Also, a major owner is less worried about being fired by the other bosses, since they own a lot of shares and have a better chance of blocking any request to leave the company.

Here is a checklist of questions you should ask yourself in order to find the leaders who avoid the short-term trap:

- Does the leader hold a significant ownership of the company?
- Does the leader's ownership in the company represent his or her biggest asset?
- Does the leader in his or her yearly letter to shareholders focus on the long-term goals or last year's success? How did these goals change in the past five to ten years?

- Does the company participate in a quarterly conference call?
- How many years has the leader led the company? What did they do before?

A lot of the answers to these questions can be found in the company's annual reports and proxy filing.

For those of you who like to entertain yourselves and want to get more insights about company leaders, transcripts of hundreds of different companies' quarterly conference calls can be found on www.seekingalpha.com (type the company name or ticker in the search box at the top left, scroll down, and look for "Earning Call Transcript").

To conclude our search for a leader, I would like to state that as investors we will be much better served with a leader who has integrity, has passion for the business, likes what he or she does, is intelligent, avoids the short-term activities trap, is a significant shareholder, and whose interests are aligned with our interests. Make up your mind about the leaders of the company by reading the annual letter, finding the leaders' incentives and ownership in the proxy filing and reading or listening to the conference calls to learn the leaders' point of view.

Let's remember that finding a leader is very important. However, even a great leader cannot save a fundamentally lousy business. As Warren Buffett said, *"When a management with a reputation for brilliance tackles a business with a reputation for poor fundamental economics, it is the reputation of the business that remains intact."*

I have now covered the first two elements of evaluating an in investment—the company itself and its leaders. In the next chapter, I will discuss the third element—the financials.

Chapter 11
The man and the olive tree

In the previous chapter, I concluded our discussion about the second of the three aspects of evaluating an investment—its leaders. One of our conclusions was that a true owner with a long-term approach will mean that company is probably a better investment than one with a leader who is an employee with only short-term incentives (and consequences).

My intention in this chapter is to discuss the financials of a company, three different ways of valuing a company and mention the three main financial statements that will help us decipher the organization's performance. I would like to emphasize one more time that knowing only the financials without understanding the company and its leaders will not get you very far.

I think the best way to start our journey into company financials is with a short story that ends with a question. Do I hear you asking why all these stories need to end with a question?

Once upon a time, there was an old man (it seems that in once-upon-a-time land there were only magical creatures, princesses in distress, and old people) who was sitting under an olive tree. The man was the owner of many olive trees (maybe ten). Over the past few decades these trees had produced plenty of olives, which the old man sold to olive oil companies who used these fine olives to manufacture their products.

However, the old man wasn't young anymore, and he dreamed of retirement on a beautiful island surrounded with orange trees. All he had to do to accomplish his dream was to figure out the value of his business and find a buyer to pay its value. There had been many people who wanted to buy his business through the years. Some wanted to cut down the trees and use the land to develop a new condo community; for them the value of the land was the value of the olive grove. Some wanted to continue to produce olives and sell them to the olive oil companies as the old man had done. Some had always dreamed of owning olive trees but were willing to pay only a figure they had in their heads instead of what it was worth.

As the old man thought about how to value his business, he came up with three different ways:

1. The value of the business is the net worth of the trees and the land.
2. The value of the business is the largest amount any buyer will be willing to pay for the trees.
3. The value of the business is the amount of cash that can be produced from selling the olives to the olive companies.

This is the question at the end of the story: what is the right way to value the old man's olive grove, and what do we need to know or look for in the financial statements of a company to determine its value?

It is important to remember that looking at the financials will only offer an insight into the company's past and near future. Understanding the organization, its competitive advantages, and its leaders will help you "see" into the long-term future.

Why do we sell low and buy high?

Let's review each one of the ways the old man used to calculate the value of his olive grove.

<u>The first way to value a company: The net worth of the trees and the land</u>

This method assumes the value of a company is the value of its tangible assets. Let's assume the old man, when starting his olive business, took a loan from the bank in order to purchase the land and the trees. Before selling the land and trees, he will need to pay back the loan to the bank; the remainder (the price for the trees minus the payback of the loan) is the value of the business.

This way of valuing a business is sometimes called "book value." Using the (simplified) accounting definition, the book value of a company is its net asset value, calculated by subtracting a company's total liabilities from the value of its total assets. For corporations the book value is often called "shareholders' equity."

Now that we've got the accounting term out of the way, let's go back to the old man. As he thought about this method of valuing his business, a young man passed by him. The old man said to the young man, "Listen, lad, I am trying to sell my olive tree business, and I came up with a great way to value it."

The young man, who was very interested in learning about businesses, asked the old man, "What is that method?"

The old man proudly said, "It's very simple, lad; the value of my business is the value of the land and the value of the trees to a tree company. For example, they can cut the trees down and use them to build furniture. The price that I get from selling the land and the trees minus the outstanding loan amount I need to pay to the bank will be the value of my business."

The young man thought for a minute and then said, "Well, I guess you decided to use the book value method of valuing your business, but there is a problem with using only the book value, especially with a cash producing business like yours."

What do you think might be the issue with using the book value as a method of valuing a business? Before continuing reading, stop for a second and see if you can answer this question. Think, lad!

One of the issues when using book value to calculate the value of a company is that book value takes into consideration only the current value of the assets and liabilities, without considering the assets' cash generation abilities. In the old man's case, every year the olive trees grow olives that are sold for cash to manufacturing companies. Since the old man's trees generate olives that can be sold for cash, the trees might be worth more than just a resource with which to create furniture. The trees have additional value as an asset that generates cash. You may remember that we previously imagined a similar situation with the rental unit; the unit is worth more than a one-time value, since it can generate rental income. For income-producing assets, the book value method might not represent the true value of the asset.

"Young lad," said the old man, "you are pretty smart! I think this method of valuing my land and trees will not represent the true value of my business. Would you be willing to help me find the true value of my olive grove?"

The young man gladly agreed, and the old man shared with him the second method of valuing his business.

Why do we sell low and buy high?

The second way to value a company: The largest amount any buyer will be willing to pay for the trees

If we consider the people looking to purchase olive tree business as buyers, and the people selling olive tree businesses as sellers, we can think of these two groups as a market for buying and selling olive tree businesses. Let's bring in our fictional Mr. Market. In this second method of valuing the olive grove, Mr. Market represents the buyers of olive tree businesses who come every day to the old man and offer him a price for his business. In this method the value of the business is the largest amount that any buyer is willing to pay for the business. This value is called the "market price."

The old man explained this method to the young man and said, "In the past three weeks, four olive tree investors offered me four different prices. I can take the highest offer and use that to represent the value of my business. What do you think, lad?"

The young man smiled and answered with a question (don't you hate when people do that?). "How will you know that the highest price is the fair price? How do you know that it is truly the fair value of your business?"

Let's stop for a second and think about it. We already know the answer, don't we? Don't forget the manic-depressive characteristics of Mr. Market and what Warren Buffett said—*"Price is what you pay; value is what you get."* We know we shouldn't confuse a company's value with its market price. As Benjamin Graham said, the market is there to serve us, not to guide us.

The young man said to the old man, "Market price (or offering) is not a measure of the value of the olive grove; it is the measure of what other people think is the price they are willing to pay for it. In order for you to make a decision whether or not to sell, you will need to estimate the value of your business as you know it to be and not be guided by other people's thoughts. That way if someone offers you a price that is greater than the value of your business, you can sell it, and until than you can wait under the trees and enjoy the olives."

The old man thanked the young man and told him, "Now I know the imperfection in using book value for income-producing assets, and I know that market price does not necessarily represent the true value of the olive grove, but I still don't know the value of my olive grove."

The young man smiled and said, "Think for a minute. Look at the last way of valuing a company."

<u>The third way to value a company: The amount of cash that can be produced by selling olives</u>

Let's go back to the definition of the intrinsic value of a company as presented in Chapters Four and Five. **The intrinsic value of a company is the discounted value of the cash that can be taken out of a business during its remaining life**. In other words, the intrinsic value of the old man's olive grove is the value of the cash that his trees generate from selling olives to olive oil companies during the business's remaining life, until the trees can't produce any more olives.

The old man's eyes opened wide. It was his turn to smile.

Before I conclude the chapter, let me leave you with a small challenge. Visit the website of any company in which you are considering investing to check out its investor relations section and pull the company's latest annual report. In the annual report, you will find the main three financial statements—the income statement (profit and loss statement), the balance sheet, and the cash flow statement.

Why do we sell low and buy high?

Study these documents and try to decide which one represents each of the three valuation methods we discussed in this chapter. Although understanding these statements is outside the scope of this book, I recommend that you read an excellent entry-level book entitled *The Accounting Game: Basic Accounting Fresh from the Lemonade Stand* by Darrell Mullis and Judith Orloff. It will give you much better insight into reading financial statements.

Chapter 12
Let it grow, let it grow, let it grow

In the previous chapter, I described three different methods of valuing a company—the book value method, the market value method, and the intrinsic value method. We also mentioned the three financial statements that help an investor understand the current financials of the organization.

My intention in this chapter is to shift our focus from a specific business investment to one key decision an investor needs to decide upon—the length of holding a stock—and the concept of compounding interest.

Before continuing, let me remind you again that the three financial statements I mentioned are the starting point in valuing a company. The statements describe the current state of the company and its past (for example, the current value of the assets that were purchased throughout the existence of the company). The statements do not predict the future, and just as we shouldn't drive a car by looking only in our rear view mirror, we shouldn't invest only by extrapolating past results into the future. Let's remember that in order to value and invest in a company, we should understand the company (and its future), its management (the leaders who will guard and grow the company's competitive advantages), and its financials (its past and current state of affairs). Along with understanding the future of the industry and the specific company, this information will enable us to make better investment decisions.

Amir Avitzur

So what is compounding interest?

Over the years many people have told me that they have compounded their investments at a great rate. However, when asked what they mean by "compounding," most people just say, "You know, it's what happens when my investment just grows significantly."

Let me explain compounding with an example. Let's assume you have $10,000 to invest. After thorough research, you have found a great company in which to invest and have done so. Assuming this investment returned 10 percent after the first year, at the end of year one your investment will be worth $11,000. If the investment continues to gain a return of 10 percent after year two, then at the end of year two it will be worth $12,100. Why is that interesting? Let's look at the numbers again. In year one, you gained $1,000 ($11,000 minus $10,000). In year two, you gained $1,100 ($12,100 minus $11,000). In both years our return was 10 percent, so what caused the difference in the dollar amount? Think for two minutes before you continue reading.

You are correct; the difference is that in year one our starting amount was $10,000, while in year two our starting amount was $11,000. That means we gained a 10 percent return **not just** on the original amount, but on the original amount **plus** the **interest** that we earned. This is referred to as compound interest.

After explaining this to one of my friends the other day, he looked a bit puzzled. "I understand the concept," he said, "but what does it matter in investing?"

Good question! Let me answer it with an example. Let's say you find a great company that grows its income at 30 percent a year and its stock price also grows by 30 percent each year (I'm allowed to come up with any fantasies I want because I'm writing the book). If you invested only $1,000 in this company, after ten years you'd end up with $13,785 if you held the investment and it compounded at 30 percent a year. Not bad, right?

Unfortunately, most investors can't hold on to a stock for even ten months, let alone ten years, so let's assume these investors sell the stock after a year, pay a 20 percent capital gain tax on their gains, and find another company with a 30 percent yearly return. Starting with the same amount of $1,000, after ten years these investors will end up with $8,594, and actually even less, since these investors will also incur trading costs.

What causes the difference?

Remember, you allowed your investment to compound at 30 percent without interfering with the growth, while the other investors stopped the growth every year, paid money out of the total funds for taxes, and then continued to compound their investment at the same rate but with a **lower** amount.

Let's have some fun. What do you think a $1,000 investment will grow to after thirty years compounding at 30 percent? How much will it be if you let it grow uninterrupted as opposed to selling it and buying into another company that grows at the same rate?

In the second case (selling and buying every year), a $1,000 investment will grow to about $634,820. I know you want to know what will be the result of the patient investor—or, as some now mockingly call us, "passive investor" (as if constant activity is superior to patience). Starting with $1,000 and paying the 20 percent capital gain tax only **once** at the end of the thirty years, this investor will be rewarded with an investment worth $2,096,196. That's quite a difference, don't you think?

Ah, the bliss of compounding. No wonder Albert Einstein, the great physicist, is widely known to have once said, *"The most powerful force in the universe is compound interest."*

For those of you who are still skeptical about the power of compound interest, let me end this chapter with a well-known story. When the Dutch settlers came to the new world, they wanted to build their town on Manhattan Island. They sent Peter Minuit (who later became the Director-General of the Dutch colony of New Netherland), representing the Dutch West India company, to purchase the island from its current owner. Tradition claims that Peter Minuit then purchased the Manhattan Island from Native Americans on May 24, 1626, for trade goods worth sixty guilders. In 1846, a New York historian converted the figure to $24, which forever remained the "magic" number of the trade.

It is interesting to note that even then governors had their issues with power. In 1631, Governor Peter Minuit was recalled back to Holland, presumably for granting privileges to the patrons at the expense of the Dutch West India Company, but as most people with power do, he recovered. A few years later, he joined the Swedish service and was given command of two vessels of mainly Swedish colonists, who established New Sweden (the first settlement on the Delaware River) in March 1638.

Let's go back to the 1626 trade. Most people think Peter Minuit and the Dutch company got the better deal. However, let's take a closer look at history with the help of compound interest.

According to the New York City Department of Finance, the total value of Manhattan property (and some major buildings in the other four boroughs) was $802.4 billion at the peak point of the real estate bubble in 2006. That figure includes also the **building value,** not just the land. You're probably thinking that Peter Minuit was the shrewdest person who ever existed. However, let's look at the Native Americans' side of the deal. If the Native Americans had taken their share of the trade ($24) and invested it at a compound rate of 6.5 percent, it would now (after 385 years) be worth a bit over $812 billion.

Hmm. Makes you think, doesn't it?

I hope this example has revealed the immensity of compound interest over a long period of time. Let's revisit my friend's question—what difference does it make in investing?

As we have seen, understanding the influence of compound interest is crucial when investing. If you find a good company with excellent growth perspective that can compound at a decent rate over many years, it is better to invest in it and let your investment return compound instead of jumping to the next big idea.

You may ask, "What do I do while it's compounding?" This is my suggestion: sit down and read more about the company. Learn whether the growth rate can continue into the future. Discover how the leaders of the company improve its competitive advantages. Observe changes in the industry that will impact the company. Research all the company's competitors and the likelihood of those competitors disrupting the company continuous growth.

When you find great companies offered at a price below their intrinsic value and with many years of growth ahead of it, it is time to *buy and hold*. You've been waiting patiently for the opportunity; when it comes, seize it. If you think study and waiting are boring, remember the 1626 trade.

Now that we have more ideas about when to buy and hold, in the next chapter I will focus on when to fold, or when to sell your investment, as well as the advantages of focus investing.

Chapter 13
When to hold them and when to fold them

In the previous chapter, I discussed the key concept of compounding and the benefits of holding a good company for a long time, letting the power of compounding interest grow our investment.

In this chapter I would like to explore the other part of being an intelligent investor—when to sell our holdings.

As I highlighted in previous chapters, the goal of the intelligent investor is to buy at a price below its intrinsic value partial ownership in a company (and it's okay to call it stocks) run by honest and capable leaders who are themselves owners of the company and have competitive advantages that can both grow and ensure the future dominance and growth of the company.

Most readers who have read all the previous chapters diligently and several times (I know you are one of these people) by now are pondering, *"Okay, so we know we should invest only in companies we understand, and we should invest only after we have done our research about the company's competitive advantages, its leaders, and its financial statement. Now we hold this great company we bought at a price below its intrinsic value, and it has been growing. When do we sell the company shares?"*

That is an excellent question. I believe one of the major mistakes that investors commit is the inability to make the right sell decision. Why can't we sell our ownership in a company?

After speaking with investors, I have learned that one of the reasons for not selling is our tendency to anchor to past prices and to extrapolate past behavior into the future. Let me give you an example to illustrate what I mean. Let's say you bought shares of a company at $10 a share. After the first year, the shares are traded at a price of $12 per share. After two years, the shares are traded at $15 per share, and after three years at $20 per share. At that point, the investor starts to believe the stock price will just continue growing and expects that the stock price will be worth $40 in five years. Surely this is no time to sell. But sometimes a strange thing happens, and after the stock reached $20 it drops back to $18. If the investor is anchored to a price of $20, he or she will not sell until the stock reaches $20 again (because it was already there). This anchoring to a past price may prevent the investor from selling the shares.

Sometimes a different scenario will happen. The same shares that reached $20 start to fall to $19, $18, $17. At some point the investor becomes so worried that the price will continue to drop that he or she sells the stock to avoid the continuous pain of watching the price drop on a daily basis.

Does this ring a bell? Has it ever happened to you? No? Think again.

Realizing these tendencies of investors, some advisors came up with a "brilliant" solution claiming to protect your profits from a big loss. These advisors recommend that investors enter a stop-loss order (An order placed with a broker to sell a security when it reaches a certain price) at 10 percent below the price of the stock. For example, if your stock is selling at $20 per share, you might enter a stop loss order for $18 per share (10 percent below the current share price). When the stock price drops to $18, it triggers the stop-loss order, and the broker sells your shares.

Let me be blunt. This idea is utter nonsense. The basis for the idea is the stock **price** and not the company **value**. If you really want to protect your profit, you will sell at $20. Why wait till the stock price drops to $18? Why do you think the above "strategy" (I'm trying to be nice) gained so many admirers and followers? The main reason is that most people do not understand the difference between the **value** of a company and the market **price** of a company. Unlike you, most people will not perform the thorough research necessary to first choose the right companies with superior management and financials and then wait till they can buy at a price below the company's intrinsic value.

Most people use only the stock price to determine whether a stock is expensive or not, thinking a $5 stock is cheaper than a $50 stock. But we know better. These people used the stop-loss order because they had no idea if $20 was a fair, overvalued, or undervalued price to pay for a company. If they gained some money, they wanted to ensure that some would be left in their pockets when the stocks were sold. I know some investors who set up a stop-loss order for every stock they buy, and in many cases all they guarantee themselves is a 10 percent loss; they buy a stock at $10 a share and issue a stop-loss order for $9, and many times the stock price goes down to $9 a share before it ever goes above $10 a share. They sell too soon.

Remembering Mr. Market and his manic-depressive characteristics, we should know that there will be times when the market will offer to buy a stock at a discount to its intrinsic value, and there will be times it will offer to buy a stock at an expensive price (above intrinsic value). It goes the other way, too; sometimes Mr. Market in his great wisdom will offer to buy a stock from you at a price that significantly exceeds its intrinsic value, and sometimes he will offer to buy a stock from you at a price that is significantly below its intrinsic value.

Light bulb! Read the last paragraph again. Yes, it is that simple and that powerful. Just as we should **buy** ownership of a company at a significant **discount** to its intrinsic value, we should **sell** our ownership of the company when it's **reaching or exceeding** its intrinsic value.

Think about it for few minutes. It does make sense. We're moving away from anchoring and obsessing over the price of the stock to focus on the value of the company. It may make your life as an investor much easier. Market prices will fluctuate daily, or even hourly. A company's intrinsic value, however, does not change so often, although it does change over time, which is the reason an investor needs to continue studying the companies he or she owns (or wants to own), as well as the competitors and the entire industry. If you know the intrinsic value of a company, you will know not only when to buy it but also when to sell it.

"Wait a second," you say. "Did you just say that if you know the intrinsic value of the company you will also know when to sell it?" Yes, that is exactly what I said. By focusing on discovering great companies and determining their intrinsic value, an investor can know the sell price before even buying shares of the company. I want to emphasize again that intrinsic value is not an exact number, and it does change over time (for example if the industry changes and the competitive advantages of the company have deteriorated), but it does not change as often as the stock price of the company, and it will enable you to make the right buy and sell decisions.

Why do we sell low and buy high?

In the next chapter, I will discuss the importance of focus investing and provide my thoughts regarding what is the "right" number of stocks to own in your portfolio.

Chapter 14
It's all about focus

In the previous chapter, I discussed the important decision of when to sell our holdings. We have been reminded again that key investment decisions should always come from knowledge about the value of the company and not from the ideas of other people (stock price) about the company. Just as we should buy ownership in a company when it is offered below its intrinsic value, we should sell our shares when their price exceeds that of the company intrinsic value.

Now that we know when to hold them and when to fold them, the next question I get from many people is, *"How many stocks should an investor own at a given time?"*

This question leads us to talk about *focus investing.*

In a 1978 letter to shareholders, Warren Buffett wrote, *"Our policy is to concentrate holdings. We try to avoid buying a little of this or that when we are only lukewarm about the business or its price. When we are convinced as to attractiveness, we believe in buying worthwhile amounts."*

The great investor Phillip Fisher wrote in his book *Common Stocks and Uncommon Profits, "The percentage of investors who own twenty-five or more different stocks is appalling. It is not this number of twenty-five or more which itself is appalling. Rather it is that in the great majority of instances only a small percentage of such holdings is in attractive stocks about which the investor has a high degree of knowledge. Investors have been so oversold on diversification that fear of having too many eggs in one basket has caused them to put far too little into companies they thoroughly know and far too much in others about which they know nothing at all. It never seems to occur to them that buying a company without having sufficient knowledge of it may be even more dangerous than having inadequate diversification."*

Read the last two paragraphs again slowly. Can you identify three key points in these quotes?

- **Concentration and knowledge**—we should **concentrate** our holdings around businesses about which we have a high degree of **knowledge**.
- **Diversification**—we are oversold on diversification.
- **Conviction**—when we find the right opportunity, we should put a significant amount of money behind it.

In previous chapters we discussed the ways to acquire **knowledge** about a company, its leaders, and its financials. Let's look now at **diversification** and **concentration**.

We are told over and over again that we should diversify our stock portfolio. Our advisors (and many money market managers) teach us that we should have as many holdings as possible to make sure that if one of our holdings drops in price our total portfolio will not be greatly affected.

It is interesting to note that most non-index stock mutual funds, who on average own shares of over a hundred distinct companies in their portfolio, underperform their equivalent index fund. However, both Warren Buffett and Phillip Fisher teach us a different lesson. Mr. Fisher tells us that *"Investors have been so **oversold** on **diversification** that fear of having too many eggs in one basket has caused them to put far too little into companies they thoroughly know and far too much in others about which they know nothing at all."*

Why do we sell low and buy high?

The key to our portfolio performance is **not** the **number** of our holdings but the knowledge and the **conviction** we have about the holdings. What is the difference between a company owner and the average investor? The average investor holds a large number of holdings (perhaps through mutual funds), about which he knows very little, for the sake of diversification. A company owner puts all his eggs in one basket (his or her company), about which they know a great deal and which they protect, guard, and grow.

Think about it. Why are we so comfortable with so many holdings? Why not invest in just a few of them?

Drawing on our previous understanding of human nature, we can identify what prevents us from making the right decision. First, of course, is our tendency to do whatever we can to avoid pain and the fear of losing. If we have a portfolio of 200 stocks and the price of one of the stocks drops by 20 percent and the rest do nothing, then our portfolio value will drop by only 0.1 percent, great, right?. Think what happens if one stock price increases by 20 percent.

The second factor combines our desire to avoid pain with our comfort in crowds. Thomas Gayner (a well regarded CIO at a major insurance company) wrote in an annual letter to shareholders, *"The inherent uncertainty in investing and thinking about the unknowable future causes people to embrace the practices of what others are doing currently. Human nature seeks comfort in crowds rather than the relative isolation of remaining independent in thoughts and actions."*

Would you rather have the same results as your close friends or be independent and underperform your friends for times in order to outperform them in the long run? How would you feel at a party at which everyone else is proclaiming how great they have been doing while your portfolio is "stuck?" Has that ever happened to you? What did you do in the tech bubble in late 1999 when all your friends invested in all sorts of dot-com companies? Were you independent in your thought and actions?

Most investor "solutions" for market uncertainty boil down to going with the crowd. As we have already mentioned, when we aren't sure what is the right behavior (or decision), our psychological tendency is to assume the people around us possess more knowledge about the situation then we do and that following their decisions will make the most sense. Combing our fear of losing (even if it's just temporarily losing face) with the market uncertainties leads us to seek the "wisdom" of the crowd. It is always more comfortable to lose together than alone. However, doing what everyone else is doing guarantees only one thing: our results will be the same as everyone else.

Gaining and using knowledge is the key. The knowledge and the understanding of investment basics give you an advantage over other investors. They have to go with the crowd because they don't know more than the people around them. You are different. As Warren Buffett wrote, *"Diversity is protection against ignorance. It makes very little sense for those who know what they're doing."*

The last idea I would like you to think about when talking about diversification is our false belief that more stocks means better diversification. I know a person who held fifty different stocks in his portfolio; however, after just a quick look, I could see that more than forty of them belonged to the medical/pharmaceutical/healthcare industry. This person did not work in the industry and did not have any more knowledge about the industry than the average investor. He truly believed he was diversified. What do you think happened to his portfolio in the mid-1990s?

Why do we sell low and buy high?

I want to emphasize again that diversification on its own is not bad. It is over-diversification across tens and hundreds of companies without knowledge that makes no sense.

So what is the right number of stocks we should hold in our portfolios?

By now I hope you can see the advantages of focusing your investment across your best ideas. What are these ideas? Let me use Benjamin Graham's words: *"An investment operation is one which, upon thorough analysis, promises safety of principal and a satisfactory return; everything else is speculation."*

Based on Mr. Graham's wisdom, your best ideas are the ones about which you are most knowledgeable, the ones on which you performed thorough analysis, and the ones that are being offered to you below their intrinsic value. These ideas will protect your principle and provide you with adequate returns.

How many of these ideas (companies to invest in) we should have in our portfolios depends on the capacity of the investor to perform the analysis. The amount of great ideas that sell below intrinsic value will usually not be large, so do a lot of research to find the few. How many companies can you really have a tremendous amount of knowledge about? Fifty? A hundred? Two hundred?

I believe that the number of holding for an individual investor with a focused portfolio is probably somewhere between ten to twenty holdings. I do not believe most individual investors can have in-depth knowledge about tens of companies and find these companies selling below their intrinsic value at the same time.

Once you have done your research and find the company offered below intrinsic value, it is important to act with **conviction**.

As Warren Buffet said, we should invest worthwhile amounts in these companies when we find them.

Think about it. Why put a little more money in your thirtieth good idea when you can put more in your best idea?

Now you might be asking, "Is twenty holdings enough to achieve diversification in my portfolio?" We need to remember that diversification has a diminishing value after x number of holdings. We can achieve over ninety percent diversification with a well-thought portfolio of twenty holdings as compared to the S&P 500 (the index of the 500 largest US corporations).

I think by now you understand that it is better to construct your portfolio with the leaders of several industries in order to achieve diversification. This will work much better than adding twenty, thirty, or forty names from each industry.

For more about the statistics behind diversification, please check out Robert Hagstorm's book *The Warren Buffett Portfolio: Mastering the power of the focus investment strategy*.

To conclude, focus investing is investing in a **select** number of companies about which you have **great knowledge**, and when given the opportunity to buy these companies at a **great price** (significantly below intrinsic value), we should act with **conviction** and put worthwhile amounts behind our decision.

Now go and focus.

Chapter 15
It is only the beginning

In the previous chapter, I discussed focus investing and the key aspects of it—concentration and knowledge, diversification, and conviction.

One of the keys to being a better investor (and some will say for a better life) is to keep on learning. To be a successful investor you need to become a learning machine (and enjoy it). As Benjamin Franklin once said, *"An investment in knowledge pays the best interest."*

Let me present a very short summary of what we have learned in this book. As you now know, to be a great investor you need not only to know what to buy and when to buy and sell; you also need to understand yourself and other investors. In the first two chapters we discussed some of the key psychological factors that prevent people from being good investors—for example, our fear of losing, our need to be liked, and our drive to do something immediately. We also talked about our overconfidence and commitment to our previous thoughts as obstacles to investment success.

From the psychological factors, we moved on to learning that a stock represents a partial ownership of a business, and I explained the dynamics of the market by introducing Benjamin Graham's manic-depressive figure Mr. Market. I emphasized Mr. Graham's teaching about Mr. Market—*"Mr. Market is there to serve you, not to guide you. It is his pocketbook, not his wisdom that you will find useful."*

I continued by explaining the key aspects of valuing a company. A company's worth is its intrinsic value, which can be defined as the discounted value of the cash that can be taken out of a business during its remaining life. In order to estimate the intrinsic value of a company, we have discovered we need to learn about the three key areas of a company—the organization, the people (the manager), and the financials. Only when we understand and can evaluate all three aspects of a company will we be ready to estimate its intrinsic value and know when to buy (and sell). In order to evaluate a company, we need to understand it. I described several key competitive advantages to look for when evaluating a company, such as pricing power, switching costs, and the network effect. We discovered some of the key questions and checklists that we should follow when researching a company.

I then moved to the second aspect of valuing a company and identified some of the qualities we need to look for when evaluating the leaders of a company. We look for managers who have ownership in the company who are honest and intelligent, and who have integrity and passion about what they do. I also described key resources that will enable us to find more information about leaders of a company.

We concluded our research by reviewing the different financials of a company, using the allegory of the old man and the olive tree to discover how to estimate the intrinsic value of a company.

The last few chapters focused on the importance of long-term investing and the power of compounding interest. I also raised the important question of when to sell a company, and we learned that the intrinsic value of a company should be used not only for the buying decision but also for the selling decision. Intrinsic value is the key.

I concluded by discussing the advantages of creating a portfolio that is concentrated on your best ideas that are selling at a price below their intrinsic value. This is what focus investing is all about. I highlighted the cornerstones of focus investing—concentration and knowledge, diversification, and conviction.

Now we have arrived at the moment you have all been waiting for—yes, more books to read! Here are my top ten favorites, in no specific order. Read them. I'm sure you will come up with your own conclusions.

1. *The Intelligent Investor* by **Benjamin Graham**
   Warren Buffett endorsed this book as "by far the best book on investing ever written." In this book you will learn more about value investing, strategies for long term success as an investor, and the principles of stock selections. Mr. Buffett advises that readers pay special attention to Chapters Eight ("The Investor and Market Fluctuations") and Twenty ("Margin of Safety").

2. *The Essays of Warren Buffett: Lessons For Corporate America* by **Lawrence Cunningham**
   This book provides a great selection of Warren Buffett's teachings as expressed in his letters to his company shareholders.

3. *You can be a stock market genius* by **Joel Greenblatt**
   Mr. Greenblatt describes and explains different areas of special situation investing. The book covers topics such as spin-offs, restructuring, options (such as LEAPS), and many more. I greatly appreciate Mr. Greenblatt's skill in providing great examples for each of the above while keeping the book exciting, sophisticated, and fun to read.

4. *The Warren Buffett Portfolio* by **Robert Hagstorm**
   Mr. Hagstorm describes the principles and philosophy behind building a concentrated portfolio and utilizes some of Mr. Buffett's investment decisions as examples. The book also covers the psychological areas of investing, as well as the mathematics behind stock selections.

5. *Common Stocks and Uncommon Profits* by **Phillip Fisher**
   The great investor Phillip Fisher wrote this book more than fifty years ago. In this book Mr. Fisher describes

ways of getting more information about companies, how to identify outstanding companies, how to determine companies' competitive advantages, and what to look for when buying a company, as well as when to sell a company and when not to. Don't miss reading part two of the book, "Conservative investors sleep well." This book is a must for those who are investing from a business point of view.

6. The *Accounting Game: Basic Accounting Fresh from the Lemonade Stand* by **Judith Orloff and Darrell Mullis**

Ignore the funny pictures. This book is a great little treasure that explains basic accounting and financial terms. You will learn about the three key financial statements and the relationship between them. It is a great beginner's book to understand accounting, the language of business.

7. *One Up On Wall Street: How to Use What You Already Know To Make Money in The Market* by **Peter Lynch**

Peter Lynch, the legendary Magellan fund manager, explains in this book how the small investor can beat the Wall Street pros by investing in individual companies. The book emphasizes through numerous examples the importance of understanding the companies you invest in, picking winners, and collecting the important facts. It provides a list of questions to ask yourself before buying a stock and identifies the best time to buy or sell a stock.

8. *The Money Game* by **Adam Smith**

In this book, written in 1976, you will get an inside look at how investors behaved in a market boom and bust, and you will learn quite a bit about the psychological nature of investors, which surprisingly enough hasn't changed in the past forty years (or, for that matter, in the past hundred years). You'll learn about the

1960s market boom, known as the Go-Go years, and the result of the unrealistic dreams of many.

9. *How to Read a Financial Report: Wringing Vital Signs Out of the Numbers* by John Tracy

   This is another valuable book about accounting and financial statements. Mr. Tracy covers the three key financial statements and explains the statements line by line, along with the relationships between them. The book also does a great job of explaining how companies can utilize the numbers to their own benefit and what to watch out for.

10. *Poor Charlie's Almanac: The Wit and Wisdom of Charles T. Munger* by Peter Kaufman

    This is not an investment book per se; however, it is a book about wisdom and human follies, and it provides great insights into the thoughts of one of the greatest investors, Warren Buffett's partner Charles Munger. I have found Chapter (or Lecture) Ten regarding the psychology of human misjudgment extremely useful in analyzing both company leaders and the behavior of stock market participants.

There are many more great books about investing and businesses. I would suggest that you also read biographies of the leaders in the industries in which you are interested. For example, if you're interested in the newspaper and media industry, you can read Katherine Graham's biography. If you're interested in the cable industry, you might want to check out *Cable Cowboy* (the story of John Malone) by Mark Robichaux. If the hotel business has your attention, you can read *The King of Cash* by Christopher Winans to learn about the Tisch family. If you're interested in the beverage industry, you might want to read *Dethroning the King* by Julie Macintosh, which deals with the takeover of the Anheuser-Busch company.

Amir Avitzur

Now that you are supported by this amazing collection of wisdom about companies, the stock market, and people, it is time to choose to grow yourself into a better investor and to capture the fruits of your learning. I hope my teachings and thoughts have helped you define and clarify your first few steps on the long and enjoyable path of becoming a stock market investor.

As a parting thought, I would like to quote Benjamin Franklin, who said, *"Do not fear mistakes. You will know failure. Continue to reach out."* When times are rough and people predict the end of the world, remember that short-term uncertainty provides to the keen investor many long-term opportunities.

Live long and prosper,
Amir Avitzur
Amir.Avitzur@AvitzurInv.com

Amir Avitzur is the president of Avitzur Asset Management, LLC, an independent money management company that has provided continuous management of investment portfolios for individuals and small businesses since 2004. Mr. Avitzur lives in New Jersey with his wife and two sons.

Important Disclosure